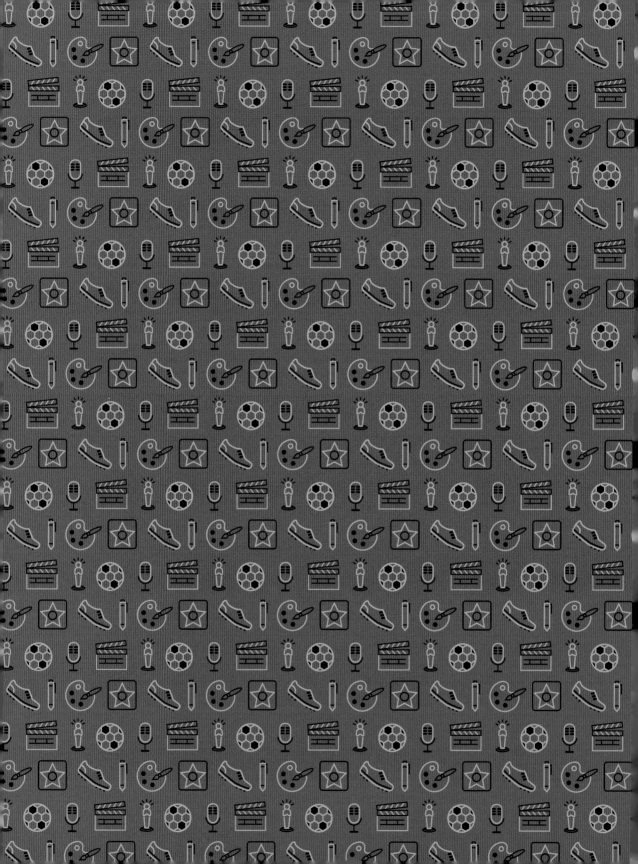

WHO DID IT FIRST?

50 ICONS, LUMINARIES, AND LEGENDS
WHO REVOLUTIONIZED THE WORLD

Henry Holt and Company, *Publishers since 1866*
Henry Holt® is a registered trademark of Macmillan Publishing Group, LLC
120 Broadway, New York, NY 10271 · mackids.com

Library of Congress Cataloging-in-Publication Data is available.
ISBN 978-1-250-26319-3

Our books may be purchased in bulk for promotional, educational, or business use.
Please contact your local bookseller or the Macmillan Corporate and Premium Sales Department
at (800) 221-7945 ext. 5442 or by email at MacmillanSpecialMarkets@macmillan.com.

First edition, 2020 / Designed by Trisha Previte
Printed in Singapore by C.O.S. Printers Pte Ltd, Singapore
1 3 5 7 9 10 8 6 4 2

WHO DID IT FIRST?

50 ICONS, LUMINARIES, AND LEGENDS
WHO REVOLUTIONIZED THE WORLD

EDITED BY
ALEX HART

WRITTEN BY
MEGAN REID

ILLUSTRATED BY
JESS CRUICKSHANK

HENRY HOLT AND COMPANY · NEW YORK

CONTENTS

INTRODUCTION

To be an icon is to be worthy of admiration and astonishment—to be the embodiment of excellence. The forty-nine iconic people (and one dog!) you'll meet in these pages come from the worlds of fashion, politics, modern art, ballet, and even space travel; all of them represent those worlds at the highest level. They're role models whose names have become synonymous with their fields. Where would American music be without the songwriting talents of Dolly Parton or Stevie Wonder? What would basketball look like without Michael Jordan, or soccer without Pelé? And how can you talk about the magic of children's books without mentioning J. K. Rowling and Harry Potter?

Carving out new spaces often means breaking the rules to change a structure from the inside out. For instance, Maya Angelou's success in publishing paved the way for other African Americans' stories to become bestsellers and reach audiences from all backgrounds. Cesar Chavez's model of engaged, peaceful advocacy for the less fortunate has become a widely adopted way that organizers create change. And by being the first person to star as a gay lead character on American network television, Ellen DeGeneres taught audiences new ways to think about the LGBTQIA+ people in their lives.

You'll find that whether they're from the past (like Jim Thorpe) or from today (like Beyoncé), many of the people in this book overcame incredible odds to achieve their dreams. It's not always easy to be the first to break new ground. But with passion and dedication, each of our icons never stopped believing that their love of an art form, a sport, or an idea could change the world.

True icons invent the worlds they want to achieve in. We hope their stories will inspire you to live your passions out loud.

JIM THORPE

THE FIRST NATIVE AMERICAN TO WIN A
GOLD MEDAL AT THE OLYMPIC GAMES (1912)

"

I was always of a restless disposition . . .

"

Jim Thorpe may well be the most extraordinary talent in the history of American sports. Born in 1888, the grandson of a great chief of the Sauk and Fox Native American nation, Jim was called Wa-Tho-Huk, or "Bright Path," by his mother. The name predicted the future that lay ahead for the young boy.

When he attended the Carlisle Indian Industrial School in Pennsylvania, everyone was amazed—this young man who had never tried the high jump, kicked a football, or thrown a javelin immediately excelled. He broke school record after record to lead the Carlisle teams to victory.

Famous football coach Pop Warner encouraged him to try out for the 1912 US Olympic track and field team, since American football was not an Olympic sport that year. Jim didn't even know what the Olympics were! At the Games in Stockholm, Sweden, he won both the pentathlon and the decathlon, breaking the world record in each event, which made him the first Native American to win an Olympic gold medal. When the king of Sweden said, "Sir, you are the greatest athlete in the world," Thorpe's reply was typical of his humility and charm: "Thanks, King," he said.

Jim went on to play professional basketball, baseball, and football, and it's estimated that during his lifetime, he mastered more than twenty sports. After he retired, he worked in films as an actor and stuntman. Even as his health declined, he was committed to helping other Native Americans in Hollywood and beyond. He was given a new name: Akapamata, or "Caregiver." Thorpe had taken his bright path to become an All-American legend.

JOSEPHINE BAKER

THE FIRST AFRICAN AMERICAN TO STAR IN A MAJOR MOTION PICTURE (1927)

> *Look out, 'cause when Josephine opens her mouth, they hear it all over the world . . .*

Born in St. Louis, Missouri, Josephine Baker escaped poverty with her dancing skills. When she moved to New York in 1924, she was quickly cast as a chorus girl in the city's famed vaudeville revues.

A year later, she traveled to Paris, France, and felt instantly at home. There, she became a superstar, iconic for her big brown eyes, famous "Banana Skirt Dance," comic timing, and pet cheetah. In 1927, she was approached to star in a French movie written just for her, titled *Siren of the Tropics*. She was the first African American person to play a lead role in any feature film, and it garnered rave reviews for its star. At a time when the biggest roles available to black actresses in America were as servants, Josephine's starring role was an aspirational one for fans. She would go on to play the lead in three more beloved films.

Josephine made her mark outside of entertainment, too. She was a spy against the Nazis, and despite living in France, she was also a voice for American civil rights. At the March on Washington in 1963, she spoke about the inequalities she had experienced: "I tell you I have walked into the palaces of kings and queens and into the houses of presidents. And much more. But I could not walk into a hotel in America and get a cup of coffee."

Josephine died four days after her last, sold-out concert. She was buried in Paris as a French military hero (the first black woman to receive these honors), and 20,000 people lined the streets of her adopted country to celebrate the history-making woman known as the "Bronze Venus."

GEORGIA O'KEEFFE

"

Making your unknown known is the important thing.

"

Georgia O'Keeffe, "the mother of American modernism," always had art in her blood: all her grandparents loved painting, as did her mother and two sisters. When she left high school, she went to study at the Art Institute of Chicago. "I found I could say things with color and shapes that I couldn't say any other way," Georgia said.

In 1907, Georgia traveled to New York and was blown away by the work she saw. She realized that photography was beginning to transform the way the world saw itself, with increased accuracy and sharpness. Georgia wanted to make her paintings mimic modern photos' realism, while experimenting with color and perspective.

But modernism was often aligned with ideas of masculinity—it was meant to be bold, brash, and brave, and Georgia was told that women were not supposed to be any of those things. She decided that the art she made was "nobody's business but [her] own." She had discovered exactly what she wanted to say with her art, and critics and collectors soon began to see the world through her eyes.

New York's Museum of Modern Art had honored male artists with exhibitions looking back at their careers, but never had a female artist been so honored . . . until Georgia in summer 1946. The fifty-seven chosen works spanned 1915 to 1945, and glowing reviews calling her the "greatest of living women painters" made the show a hit with the public. With the retrospective, she paid tribute to the Southwestern vistas, plants, and flowers she loved to paint and her family of artists who nurtured her dreams. Georgia painted until the day she died, in 1986 at age ninety-eight.

NAT KING COLE

THE FIRST AFRICAN AMERICAN TO HOST
A NATIONAL TELEVISION SHOW (1956)

Nathaniel Adams Coles became Nat King Cole the singer almost by accident. He got his famous nickname when an audience member placed a paper hat on his head and called him "Old King Cole." And he only began to sing after a wealthy patron who enjoyed Nat's jazz trio demanded it.

Nevertheless, Nat was a born performer. A minister's son from Montgomery, Alabama, he was playing the piano by age four, toured the country with the first all-black Broadway show at seventeen, and released an album at twenty-one. In 1956, at age thirty-seven, Nat was offered the chance to host a television show on NBC. By then, he had recorded fourteen albums and had three number-one singles. He captivated audiences young and old with his swinging style and emotive baritone. It only made sense that Nat's charm and charisma should reach the living rooms of millions of Americans.

Nat was a natural on TV, cracking jokes, leading interviews, and singing to a live studio audience. And importantly, he was the first African American to host a national talk show. Critics and fans loved him.

Still, while the show had advertising sponsors in some cities, some stations didn't air *The Nat King Cole Show* because of Nat's race. In 1957, he decided to stop filming because, as he said, advertisers were "afraid of the dark."

But that was far from the end of Nat's career. He went on to record over two dozen more albums, and continued to perform until he died of cancer at forty-five. And in a twist he never could've imagined, he became number one once more in 1991 with the posthumous release of a track with his daughter Natalie.

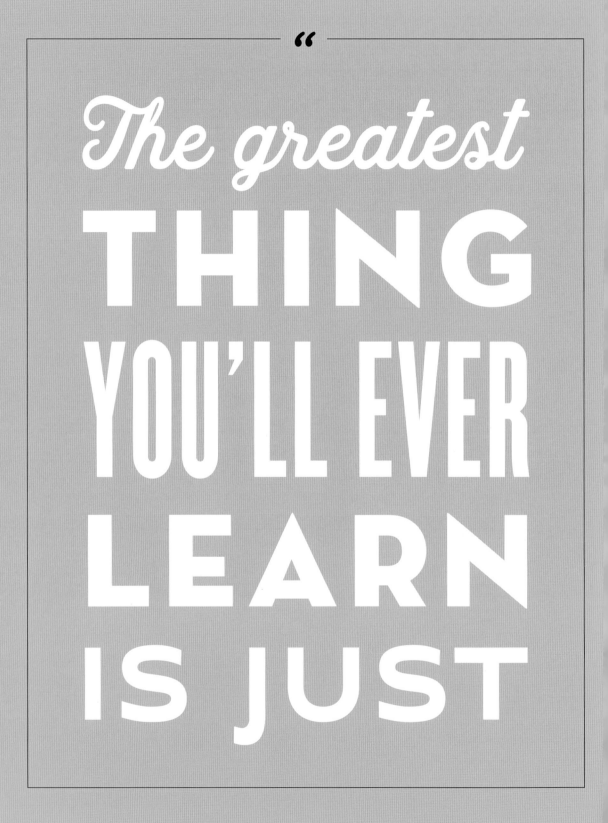

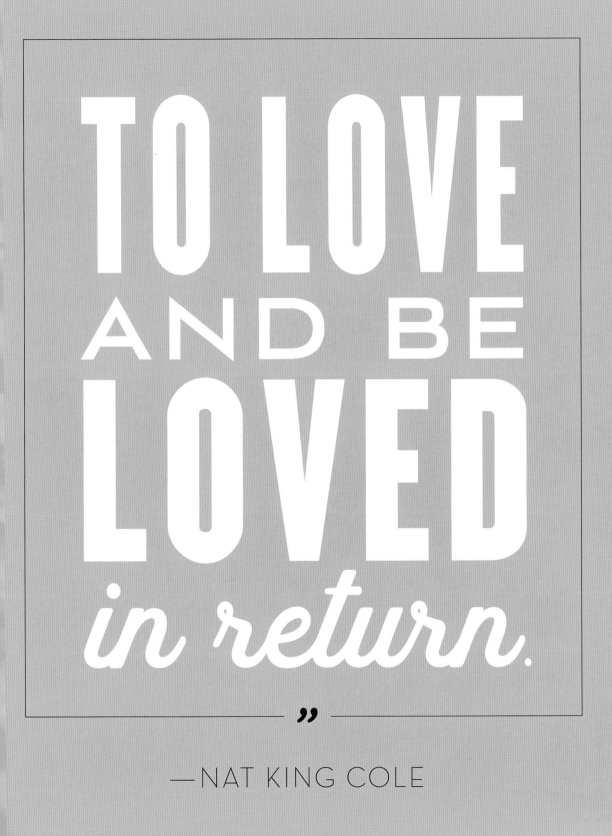

TO LOVE
AND BE
LOVED
in return.

"

—NAT KING COLE

LAIKA

THE FIRST LIVING CREATURE TO ORBIT THE EARTH (1957)

"

Gav-gav! (or "Woof!" in Russian)

"

The first creature to take a trip around our planet in space was a "very good girl" named Laika, a terrier-mix stray dog from the streets of Moscow, Russia. The compact eleven-pound Laika was originally called Kudryavka, or "Little Curly," for her spiral tail and half-cocked ears. But when she was introduced to the country via radio, she woofed a cheerful "hello," causing her to be renamed Laika, or "barker."

Scientists wanted to send humans to space. But they first needed to understand what effects space flight and g-forces would have on a body and brain. They decided to send another mammal—namely, Laika—for research. Veterinarians monitored Laika's blood pressure, heart rate, and other factors that would predict her survival. Finally three-year-old Laika was ready. She even had her own canine space suit. At five thirty a.m. on November 3, 1957—four years before her countryman Yuri Gagarin became the first human in space—Laika blasted off in a shuttle called Sputnik 2 and became the world's first cosmonaut.

She was probably frightened in the small spacecraft (despite the supply of snacks), unable to understand the loud noises as she was catapulted beyond the Earth's atmosphere. But soon, she could see farther than any earthling had before as she orbited our blue and green planet.

Sometime after her fourth orbit, scientists stopped receiving data from Laika's sensors. Tragically, they discovered that the spacecraft had overheated. Laika did not survive her history-making flight. She never chose her fate, but her selfless sacrifice helped prepare humans to explore our infinite universe. An enduring, furry symbol of bravery and scientific achievement, Laika is the ultimate icon of space exploration.

JUDY GARLAND

THE FIRST WOMAN TO WIN THE GRAMMY AWARD
FOR ALBUM OF THE YEAR (1962)

"

Always be a first-rate version of yourself,
instead of a second-rate version of someone else.

"

Imagine "the greatest night in show business history." It would have to be at a famous venue, featuring works by some of the best composers. The crowd would be composed of screaming fans, whipped into a frenzy by a world-class orchestra. And most importantly, it would need a renowned celebrity.

On April 23, 1961, those stars aligned at Carnegie Hall in New York City, when Judy Garland performed what critics have called the best live concert of all time. Luckily, it was recorded as *Judy at Carnegie Hall*. It became the first album by a woman to win the Grammy Award for Album of the Year, in addition to three other Grammy Awards. It spent thirteen weeks at number one on the Billboard music charts.

Judy's Carnegie Hall concert only

cemented her status as an entertainment legend. Born Frances Ethel Gumm in 1922, she had been famous for nearly all her life—she had been performing since the age of two and a half! Best known for her roles in *The Wizard of Oz* (1939) and *Meet Me in St. Louis* (1944), Judy took on many roles that showcased both her acting prowess and rich singing voice.

That night at Carnegie Hall was not only a tribute to her career, but a thank-you to the fans who had stayed by her side through hard times. "I'm a woman who wants to reach out and take forty million people in her arms," she said. Like many stars who've attained the status of icon, Judy's kindness melded with her talents to touch her viewers', and listeners' hearts—while making history in the process.

STEVIE WONDER

"

*Music is a world within itself,
with a language we all understand.*

"

Some icons spend decades attempting to achieve their "first," but Stevie Wonder earned his before he started high school! Born Stevland Hardaway Judkins in 1950, Stevie was quickly labeled a musical prodigy. He taught himself the harmonica, drums, and piano by ten years old and loved to sing in the church choir.

In 1961, he released his first record with the famous Motown label, and "Little Stevie Wonder" was born. In 1963, a live performance of his single "Fingertips, Pt. 2" became a sensation. And when he was thirteen years old, he ascended to number one on the Billboard Hot 100 chart.

Over the next decade, he released hit after hit. He deepened his artistry by writing and producing (overseeing vocal and instrumental recordings and coaching artists in the studio) for other artists. Stevie was born without his eyesight, so he navigated the worlds of funk, soul, electronica, R & B, pop, and jazz all without reading music or formal lessons. He never felt held back by his blindness: "Being blind, you don't judge books by their covers."

In 1976, Stevie released *Songs in the Key of Life*, widely regarded as his masterpiece. It was the first album by an American artist to debut at number one on the Billboard charts. Soulful, now-classic pop songs like "I Just Called to Say I Love You" (1984) and "Overjoyed" (1985) followed. To date, Stevie has had ten number one Billboard singles; he's also sold over 100 million records. With twenty-five Grammys, he is the solo artist with the most of the coveted awards.

ELLA FITZGERALD

**THE FIRST WOMAN TO WIN A GRAMMY
LIFETIME ACHIEVEMENT AWARD (1967)**

"It isn't where you came from. It's where you're going that counts.

One night at the Apollo Theater in Harlem in New York City, a young girl named Ella prepared to dance. She had had a hard childhood—abandoned by her father, left homeless when her mother died, sent to harsh boarding schools, and mistreated by the adults in her life—but she often made money by dancing on the streets in her neighborhood. Ella thought she had a good chance of winning the prize. But then she saw her competition. Suddenly nervous, she decided to sing for the crowd instead.

It was our good luck that she did. After a triumphant win that night in 1934, Ella Fitzgerald went on to become perhaps the most influential singer in American jazz. She was called "The First Lady of Song," and her career spanned decades, genres, and continents. She was known for the sweetness of her tone in ballads like "Someone to Watch Over Me," as well as for her ability to mimic the horns in her backing bands in swing classics like "Airmail Special." She helped define what jazz could be, and with about 40 million albums sold, she brought the genre into the homes of millions of Americans.

In her career, Ella won thirteen Grammy Awards and was nominated twenty times. She is the female artist with the most recordings in the Grammy Hall of Fame. Because of her many achievements, she was given the Recording Academy's Lifetime Achievement Award in 1967, an award given only to artists who have had a lasting impact on the field of recording. She was the first woman to win it, but not the last. To date, there are more than thirty women who have received the honor.

SHIRLEY CHISHOLM

THE FIRST AFRICAN AMERICAN WOMAN
ELECTED TO CONGRESS (1968)

For seven terms between 1969 and 1983, Shirley Chisholm was an outspoken advocate for the American ideals of freedom and equality in the United States House of Representatives.

But she certainly never dreamed of being the first African American woman in Congress when she was a young girl in Brooklyn, New York. She was born to Caribbean immigrants in 1924 and excelled in school. As a college debating champion, she was encouraged by her professors to use her keen mind and persuasive speaking skills to enter politics, but Shirley wasn't convinced. The oldest of four sisters, she was comfortable with children, so she earned her master's degree in childhood education from Columbia University and worked in nursery schools and on education policy.

Still, Shirley stayed engaged in local politics and was involved with her local League of Women Voters and branch of the Democratic Party. When her neighborhood of Bedford-Stuyvesant in Brooklyn, New York, became its own voting district, she knew that the time was right for her to run for office. In 1968, she ran for Congress on the motto "Unbought and Unbossed," and won over her rival by a margin of about two to one, making her the very first African American woman elected to Congress.

"Fighting Shirley" quickly made her mark as a fierce advocate for veterans' rights, education, benefits for women and children, and national security. And in 1972, Shirley embodied another "first" by becoming the first black person and the first woman to run for the Democratic Party's presidential nomination. A role model for generations of feminists, activists, and politicians to come, she made change as, in her words, "a black woman who lived in the twentieth century and dared to be herself."

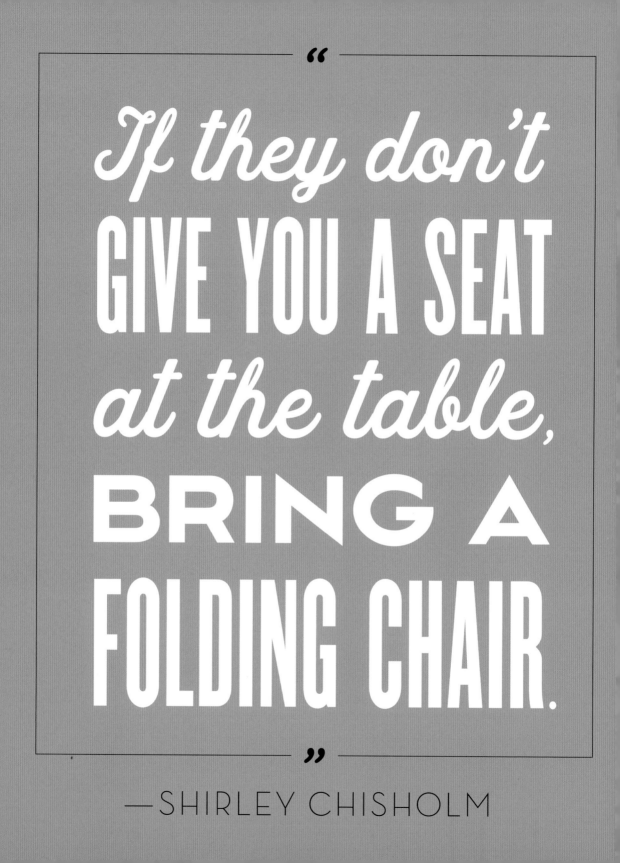

" If they don't GIVE YOU A SEAT at the table, BRING A FOLDING CHAIR. "

—SHIRLEY CHISHOLM

TURN THE PAGE TO MEET SOME

POLITICAL ICONS

in the making

SADIQ KHAN
FIRST MUSLIM MAYOR
OF LONDON (2016)

ALEXANDRIA OCASIO-CORTEZ
FIRST WOMAN UNDER THE AGE OF
30 TO BE ELECTED TO THE UNITED
STATES CONGRESS (2018)

SHARICE DAVIDS AND DEB HAALAND
FIRST NATIVE AMERICAN WOMEN
ELECTED TO CONGRESS (2018)

RASHIDA TLAIB AND ILHAN OMAR
FIRST MUSLIM WOMEN ELECTED
TO CONGRESS (2018)

KARINA GOULD
FIRST WOMAN UNDER THE AGE
OF 30 TO SERVE AS A CABINET
MEMBER IN CANADA (2017)

JORDON STEELE-JOHN
FIRST SENATOR UNDER THE AGE OF
25 TO SERVE IN THE AUSTRALIAN
PARLIAMENT (2017)

GEORGINA BEYER
FIRST OPENLY TRANSGENDER MEMBER
OF PARLIAMENT IN NEW ZEALAND (1999)

POLITICAL ICONS IN THE MAKING

 GEORGINA BEYER (born 1957) is a New Zealand politician who became the world's first openly transgender Member of Parliament in 1999. During that election, Georgina surprised many by winning the then right-leaning Wairarapa electorate with a majority vote. Through her political work, Georgina strives to make New Zealand a safer and more accepting place for all members of the LGBTQIA+ community.

 SADIQ KHAN (born 1970) is a British politician who became the first Muslim mayor of London in 2016. The son of first-generation immigrants from Pakistan, Sadiq earned a law degree from the University of North London. He worked as a solicitor specializing in human rights issues, and he has made immigration policy a focal point of his political work. In 2018, Sadiq was included on the *Time* 100 list, an annual list of the most influential people in the world.

 JORDON STEELE-JOHN (born 1994) is an English-born Australian politician who became the youngest member of Australian parliament in 2017. Due to cerebral palsy, Jordon uses a wheelchair. He has used his position to advocate for disability rights and young people alike. In 2018, Jordon announced that he would attempt to pass a bill that would lower the voting age in Australia to sixteen, giving younger Australians the right to vote and have a say in their country's future.

KARINA GOULD (born 1987) is a Canadian politician who became the youngest female cabinet minister in 2017 and the first federal cabinet minister to give birth while in office in 2018. Having previously worked for the Organization of American States as a consultant on their Migration and Development team, she is a trade and investment specialist and community activist. She has focused her work on advocating for women's rights and affordable housing.

SHARICE DAVIDS (born 1980) is an American politician and lawyer who, alongside Deb Haaland, is one of the first Native American women elected to Congress in 2018. She is also the first openly LGBTQIA+ Native American woman elected to Congress, and the first openly LGBTQIA+ person elected to Congress from Kansas. She is a member of the Ho-Chunk (Winnebago) Nation, whose historic territory is Wisconsin, Minnesota, Iowa, and Illinois. Sharice also happens to be a former professional mixed martial artist!

DEB HAALAND (born 1960) is an American politician who, alongside Sharice Davids, is one of the first Native American women elected to Congress. In 2018, Deb was elected to represent New Mexico's first congressional district. She is a member of the Laguna Pueblo people, whose historic territory is New Mexico. Representing her people, Deb wore a traditional Pueblo dress, necklace, and boots to her congressional swearing-in on January 3, 2019. In March of that year, Deb became the first Native American woman to preside over the United States House of Representatives.

ALEXANDRIA OCASIO-CORTEZ (born 1989) is an American politician and activist who became the youngest woman ever elected to Congress in 2018, representing New York's fourteenth congressional district. As a member of the Democratic Socialists of America, Alexandria focuses her work and advocacy around progressive and liberal left-wing causes, such as social justice and egalitarianism. The MIT Lincoln Library named an asteroid after her for placing second in the 2007 Intel International Science and Engineering Fair.

 ILHAN OMAR (born 1982) is an American politician who, alongside Rashida Tlaib, is one of the first two Muslim women elected to Congress in 2018. Ilhan is also the first Somali American congressperson, the first naturalized citizen from Africa serving in Congress, and the first woman of color elected to represent Minnesota in Congress. Ilhan is a member of the Congressional Progressive Caucus and is known for advocating for progressive initiatives like student loan debt forgiveness, affordable housing, universal health care, and abolishing US Immigration and Customs Enforcement (ICE).

 RASHIDA TLAIB (born 1976) is an American politician and lawyer. In 2018, she was elected to the United States House of Representatives, representing Michigan's thirteenth congressional district. Rashida is the first Muslim woman to serve in the Michigan legislature, the first Palestinian American woman to serve in Congress, and (with Ilhan Omar) one of the first two Muslim women elected to Congress. Along with Alexandria Ocasio-Cortez, Rashida is a member of the Democratic Socialists of America and focuses her policy work on left-leaning initiatives like domestic policy reform in regard to universal health care and immigration reform. She's the eldest of fourteen children!

"

It's never TOO EARLY TO START... HELPING OTHER PEOPLE. *If you work hard,* PEOPLE WILL REMEMBER THAT.

"

—DEB HAALAND

PELÉ

"

It doesn't matter if you are rich, or poor, or black, or white. [Soccer] is one nation.

"

Edson Arantes do Nascimento's whole family was excited when it was time for Brazil to play Uruguay in the 1950 World Cup. But when Brazil lost the match, Edson's father couldn't help but cry with frustration. Seeing his dad's tears, the nine-year-old promised, "Don't cry, don't cry, I'm going to win the World Cup for you."

By then, Edson was already being called Pelé by his friends and family. He was also beginning to love soccer. When he was fifteen, his father took him to try out for the professional Santos Football Club. His first season with Santos FC, Pelé became the top scorer in the league. By 1958, when he was four months shy of eighteen, he made good on his childhood promise by helping his team win the FIFA World Cup. Brazil won again in 1962 and

1970, making Pelé the only player to win three of these international championships.

Pelé quickly became one of the best-known soccer players in the world. His skills seemed supernatural, beyond humanly possible. It was almost as if he could communicate with the ball, steering it effortlessly into goal after goal after goal.

On November 19, 1969, Brazilians tuned in to watch Pelé's team, Santos, against Vasco da Gama, in hopes of seeing Pelé make O Milésimo, or "The Thousandth" goal. And he did just that, in a penalty kick. He was the first player to score that many goals in his career, but he didn't stop there. According to FIFA, Pelé is still the top league goal-scorer in the entire world, with 1,281 points earned in 1,363 games before he retired in 1977.

MAYA ANGELOU

THE FIRST AFRICAN AMERICAN TO WRITE A *NEW YORK TIMES* BESTSELLING BOOK (1970)

Writing about Dr. Maya Angelou's life is a daunting prospect when what she is best known for is her autobiography *I Know Why the Caged Bird Sings*. The first book by a black person to be a *New York Times* bestseller, the story of Maya's childhood and adolescence has sold over 100 million copies and has been translated into seventeen languages since its publication in 1969. She went on to write six more books about her life.

Maya was born in St. Louis, Missouri, in 1928 and moved to Stamps, Arkansas, at age three. The South was deeply segregated at the time, and it could be dangerous to be a young black girl. In addition to the dangers racism posed, Maya was molested at age eight and didn't speak for five years. But discovering books, poetry, and the power of her bright mind helped her reclaim her voice.

Maya went on to have a big life. She was a singer, a film writer (she was also the first black woman writer whose screenplay was turned into a film!), a mother, a dancer, a magazine editor, and a college professor—among many other jobs. In addition to the seven books about her life, she wrote twenty-nine other works—thirty of which were bestsellers.

With her first bestselling book, Maya proved that the African American experience was just as compelling and important to read about as white people's lives—and that works by and about black folks could be just as successful. In *I Know Why the Caged Bird Sings*, the humanity of black people was impossible to ignore—as were the strong spirit and powerful voice of one of America's most beloved writers.

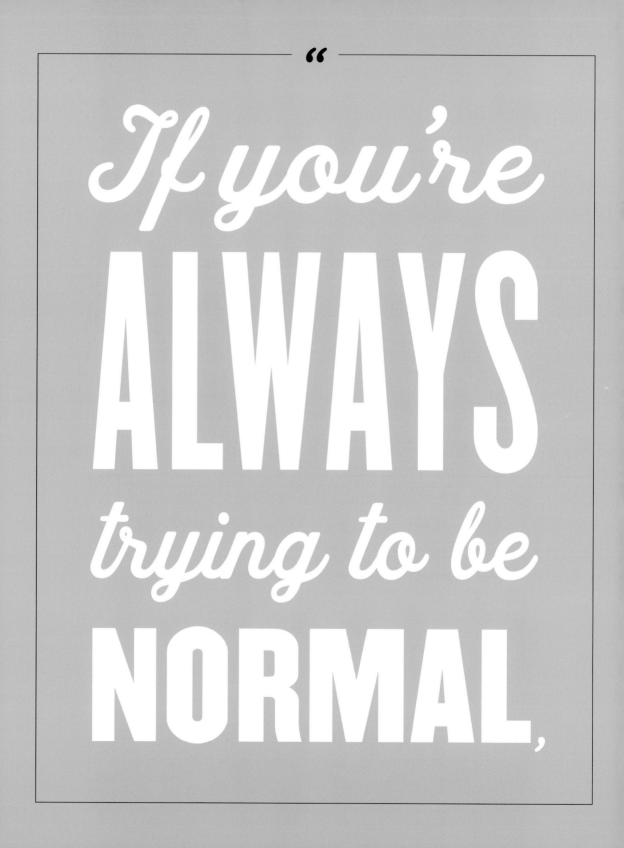

"

If you're
ALWAYS
trying to be
NORMAL,

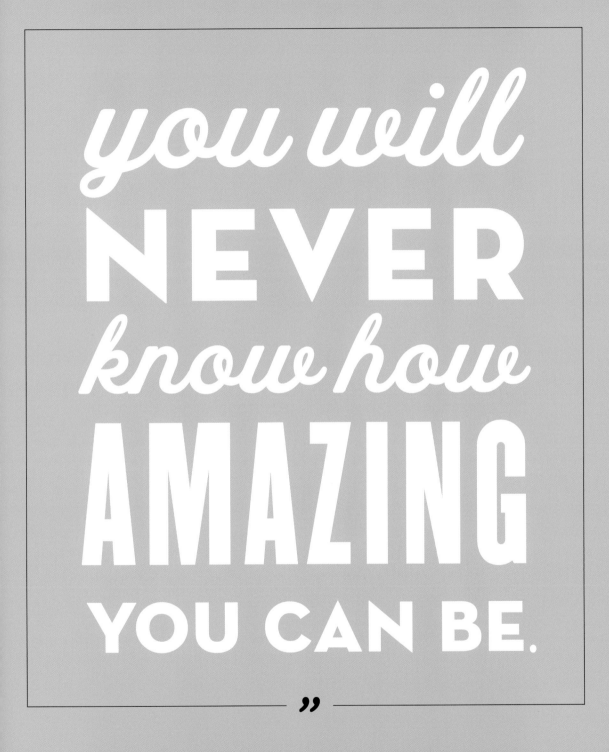

you will NEVER know how AMAZING YOU CAN BE.

"

—MAYA ANGELOU

STEPHEN HAWKING

THE FIRST PERSON TO EXPLAIN THE COSMOS USING THE GENERAL THEORY OF RELATIVITY AND QUANTUM MECHANICS (1973)

"
Our goal is nothing less than a complete description of the universe we live in.
"

Stephen Hawking's teachers in grade school would have told you that he was just a middling student, often bored and more interested in model airplanes and early computers than homework. But by high school, his genius began to show. He loved math and theoretical thinking, so he pursued physics and chemistry at England's Oxford University.

His graduate studies led him to cosmology, the study of the universe. In 1973, Stephen decided to apply quantum theory (which studies particles smaller than atoms) and Einstein's theory of relativity (which accounts for the relationship between energy and mass) to the idea of black holes. To his surprise, physics proved that instead of being voids, black holes actually morphed and changed, evidence that space is actively expanding. For the first time, scientists could imagine how our galaxy was created.

But back on Earth, the researcher battled amyotrophic lateral sclerosis, also called ALS or Lou Gehrig's disease, which he had been diagnosed with in 1963. Eventually, Stephen could move only his eyes and a finger, and he used a breakthrough speech synthesizer to turn his eye movements into words. By the time he died in 2018, his life had become a shining example of his deep belief "that people need not be limited by physical handicaps as long as they are not disabled in spirit." A cultural icon and family man, as well as a talented physicist, Stephen inspired millions of people through his appearances on television and radio shows, many books, and several films made about his life.

EDITH HEAD

THE FIRST PERSON TO WIN EIGHT
ACADEMY AWARDS IN COSTUME DESIGN (1974)

"

Clothes are the way you present yourself to the world;
they affect the way the world feels and thinks about you;
subconsciously they affect the way you feel and think about yourself.

"

In 1924, Edith Head was a teacher living in Hollywood after getting her master's degree in romance languages at Stanford University. She heard that a film studio was hiring a costume sketch artist to work with the director Cecil B. DeMille. Edith had taken a few art classes, and she had made costumes for her pets as a child—she was later quoted as saying, "Anyone who can dress a horn toad, can dress anything!"—so she thought she'd give it a shot.

Edith got the job. She had an eye for fit and proportion, and more importantly, she helped pioneer the idea that clothing could reflect character. A particular hat or skirt could help actors move and even think like the characters they were portraying, whether Egyptian servants or outlaws.

The Academy of Motion Picture Arts and Sciences took note, awarding Edith her first Academy Award in 1950 for *The Heiress*. By the end of her career, Edith had accumulated eight Academy Awards. She still holds the record for the most Oscars in costume design, and with thirty-five nominations over her career, is the most nominated woman in Oscar history.

Edith had a big impact on the world of fashion beyond Hollywood. Her designs were beloved because they crossed over easily into real life. In fact, pieces Edith designed, like the skinny black pants Audrey Hepburn wore in *Sabrina* or the cropped tops showcased in *The Lady Eve* and *Samson and Delilah*, continue to influence styles today.

HARVEY MILK

THE FIRST OPENLY GAY CANDIDATE TO WIN
AN ELECTION IN CALIFORNIA (1977)

"

Rights are won only by those who make their voices heard.

"

Born in 1930, Harvey Milk was known as one of Woodmere, New York's class clowns. He was always confident, but for many years, he wasn't sure what to do with his life. In 1972, he moved to San Francisco, where his life in politics would begin.

First he opened a shop called Castro Camera, which became a hub for LGBT activists to gather. From there, he began organizing groups to support the neighborhood's schools, businesses, and citizens. He was proud of the change he was effecting and wanted to do more. At the time, there were almost no openly gay politicians, but Harvey wasn't deterred. In 1973 and 1975, he ran to join the city's board of supervisors. Both times Harvey narrowly lost, but each failure taught him more and more. "I know the rules of their game now and how to play it."

His persistence paid off. On November 8, 1977, Harvey beat sixteen other candidates to become one of San Francisco's city supervisors, making him the first openly gay person to win an election in California.

Not everyone was pleased. About a year after Harvey was sworn in, he and Mayor George Moscone were assassinated. As the nation mourned, the brave words he recorded in his will became a rallying cry for gay rights around the country: "If a bullet should enter my brain, let that bullet destroy every closet door." Today, Harvey Milk is admired as an American hero, not just for his activism in the queer community, but for his belief that every citizen can—and should—strive to make their corner of the world a better, more inclusive place.

RITA MORENO

THE FIRST PERSON OF COLOR TO EGOT (1977)

As a girl, Rita loved to sing and dance for her grandfather. When she moved from Puerto Rico to New York in the mid-thirties, where her seamstress mother had taken a job in a sweatshop, Rita was heartbroken to leave her extended family. But the move helped her make her dreams come true. At age eleven, she was already recording voice-over tracks for films, and at thirteen, she landed her first Broadway role, in *Skydrift*.

Rita was hardworking, beautiful, and skilled. But she struggled to find roles for non-white women like her that weren't merely portraying stereotypes such as maids. Finally, in 1961, thirty-year-old Rita was cast as Anita in the film version of *West Side Story*. She not only lit up the screen with her dancing but also was able to portray empathy, humor, and wisdom through her acting—and best of all, Anita was a Puerto Rican New Yorker, just like her. Rita won the Academy Award (also called the Oscar—the highest award in movies) for Best Supporting Actress for her work in *West Side Story*. It was the first of many major awards she would accumulate. In 1977, she became the first Latinx (and only the third person) to win the awards that make up a coveted EGOT—an Emmy (for *The Muppet Show* in 1977), a Grammy (for her recordings for *The Electric Company* in 1972), an Oscar (1962), and a Tony (for *The Ritz* in 1975).

People still made assumptions about Rita because of where she came from and what she looked like. In fact, she wasn't cast in another major film for seven years after *West Side Story*. But Rita became a role model for a generation of brown actresses who dreamed of playing strong, independent characters on-screen. "When I see a young woman acting in a way that says, 'I have value, I am worthy,'" she said in 2019, "it just moves me to tears because I never thought I would see that day happen."

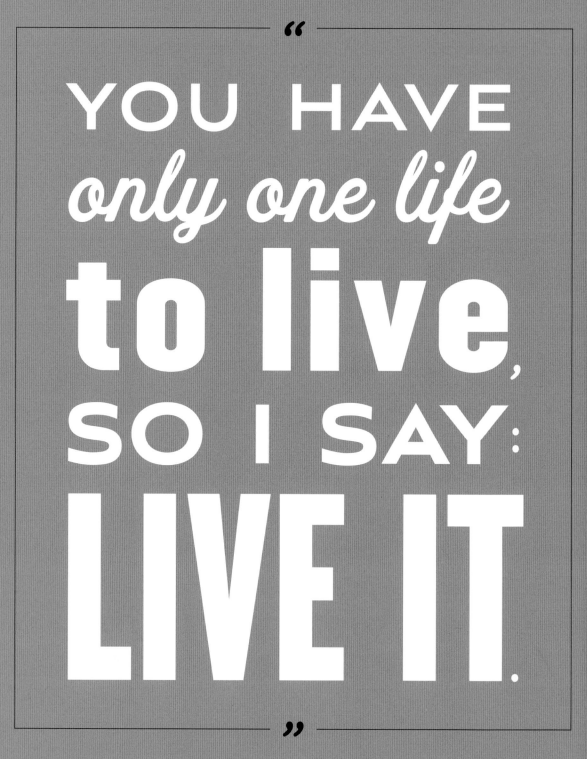

" YOU HAVE *only one life* to live, SO I SAY: LIVE IT. "

—RITA MORENO

TURN THE PAGE TO MEET SOME OTHER

EGOT WINNERS

JOHN LEGEND
FIRST AFRICAN AMERICAN
MAN TO EGOT (2018)

HELEN HAYES
FIRST WOMAN TO EGOT
(1977)

RICHARD RODGERS
FIRST PERSON TO EGOT
(1962)

WHOOPI GOLDBERG
FIRST AFRICAN AMERICAN
TO EGOT (2002)

MEL BROOKS
FIRST WRITER TO EGOT
(2001)

ROBERT LOPEZ
FIRST FILIPINO AMERICAN
TO EGOT (2014)

EGOT WINNERS

RICHARD RODGERS (1902–1979) was an American composer and the first person ever to win at least one Emmy, Grammy, Oscar, and Tony Award. Richard was best known for his compositions for musical theater. In 1946, he won an Oscar for the song "It Might as Well Be Spring" from the film *State Fair*. In 1950, he won multiple Tony Awards for the musical *South Pacific*. His Grammy came in 1960, thanks to the soundtrack for *The Sound of Music*. Finally, in 1962, Richard won an Emmy for the music in the ABC documentary *Winston Churchill: The Valiant Years*.

HELEN HAYES (1900–1993) was an American actress who was given the nickname "First Lady of American Theatre." In 1977, she became the first woman to EGOT. Helen began her EGOT journey in 1931 with an Oscar for her role in *The Sin of Madelon Claudet*. For the role of Addie in *Happy Birthday*, Helen won a Tony in 1947. Next, she received an Emmy in 1953 for her role on *Schlitz Playhouse of Stars*. She completed her EGOT by winning a Grammy in 1977 for her work on the spoken-word album *Great American Documents*.

MEL BROOKS (born 1926) is an American filmmaker, writer, comedian, actor, and composer. He is the first writer to complete an EGOT. He won the Emmy for Outstanding Writing Achievement in Variety in 1967 for *The Sid Caesar, Imogene Coca, Carl Reiner, Howard Morris Special*. Soon after, in 1969, Mel won the Best Original Screenplay Oscar for *The Producers*. In 1998, Mel won a Grammy for his album *The 2000 Year Old Man in the Year 2000*. Finally, in 2001, Mel won three Tony Awards, including Best Book of a Musical, for *The Producers*, an adaptation of his film.

WHOOPI GOLDBERG (born Caryn Elaine Johnson in 1955) is an American comedian, actress, television personality, producer, and author. After getting her start in avant-garde theater, Whoopi was the star of the one-woman Broadway show *Whoopi Goldberg*. The recording of her performance in that show won her a Grammy in 1985. In 1991, Whoopi won an Oscar for her performance in the film *Ghost*. Whoopi's performance in the television special *Beyond Tara: The Extraordinary Life of Hattie McDaniel* won her an Emmy in 2002. And in that same year she became the first African American to EGOT after receiving a Tony for producing the revival of the musical *Thoroughly Modern Millie*.

ROBERT LOPEZ (born 1975) is an American songwriter. He is the first Filipino American to achieve EGOT status and the first person to EGOT twice. In 2004, he won a Tony Award for *Avenue Q*, and then won another in 2011 for *The Book of Mormon*. Between winning those two Tony Awards, he won two Emmys (in 2008 and 2010) for his work on the television show *Wonder Pets!* In 2011, he won a Grammy for *The Book of Mormon*, and then won another for *Frozen* in 2014. And he finished his first EGOT with an Oscar for *Frozen* in 2014 (making him the first Filipino American to ever win an Academy Award); his second EGOT was achieved with an Oscar for *Coco* in 2018.

JOHN LEGEND (born John Roger Stephens in 1978) is an American singer, songwriter, actor, producer, and philanthropist. Following the release of his first album, John won a Grammy for Best New Artist in 2006. John won an Oscar in 2015 for "Glory," which was featured in the movie *Selma*. Following his success in music and film, John took to the theater world and won a Tony in 2017 for co-producing the August Wilson play *Jitney*. And in 2018, John won an Emmy for co-producing a live television broadcast of the musical *Jesus Christ Superstar* (which he also starred in), becoming the first African American man to EGOT.

GEORGE BALANCHINE

THE FIRST CHOREOGRAPHER TO WIN A KENNEDY CENTER LIFETIME ACHIEVEMENT AWARD (1978)

Georgi Balanchivadze was born in Russia in 1904. When he was only thirteen, his family left him there to train as a dancer while they returned to their homeland, the country of Georgia. As an adult, he dreamed of creating a space where young dancers could thrive and feel part of a family. In 1948, New York's City Center offered George Balanchine, as he was now known, his own permanent company to be housed in their complex. He leaped at the chance. His dancers adored him (nicknaming him "Mr. B"), and it is estimated that he choreographed 465 ballets in his lifetime.

George's new (and sometimes shocking!) ideas for what ballet could be made him perhaps the most famous choreographer of all time. His works didn't have complex plots; instead, in ballets like *Serenade* and *Jewels*, George relied on careful choreography and his dancers' meticulous training to evoke emotion. The dramatic pliés and extreme arabesques in his dances drew on strict technique while allowing the New York City Ballet's dancers' individual skills to shine.

The Kennedy Center for the Performing Arts in Washington, DC, holds an annual gala honoring the most influential creative people in the country. Balanchine had turned ballet upside down, and everyone agreed the art was better for it. The man who had once been a lonely young dancer became the first choreographer to be honored with the Kennedy Center's Lifetime Achievement Award in 1978. Accepting his award, perhaps George thought of one of his favorite sayings when he was honored for a lifetime of hard work: "Ballet is important and significant—yes. But first of all, it is a pleasure."

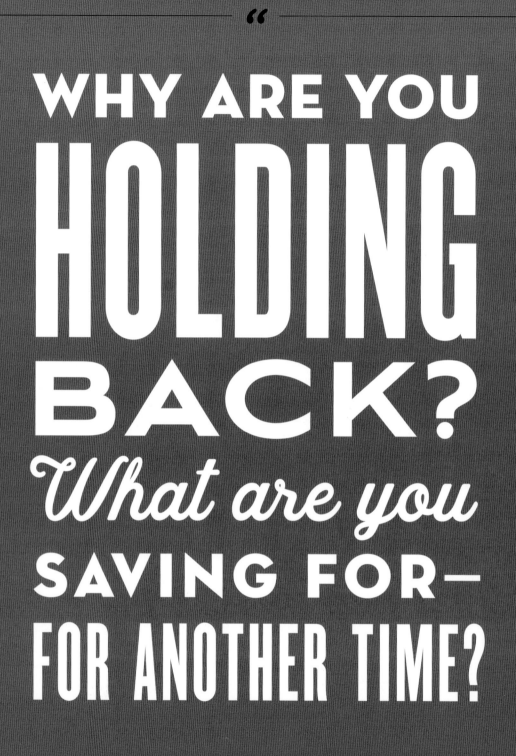

"

WHY ARE YOU
HOLDING
BACK?
What are you
SAVING FOR—
FOR ANOTHER TIME?

There are not OTHER TIMES. THERE IS ONLY NOW.

"

—GEORGE BALANCHINE

FLORENCE "FLOJO" GRIFFITH JOYNER

THE FIRST WOMAN TO RUN THE 100-METER DASH
IN UNDER 10.5 SECONDS (1988)

Was young Delorez Florence Griffith always destined to be "FloJo," the fastest woman in the world? Her mother certainly thought so. "We called her 'Lightning' because when she started to walk . . . she ran all through the house," she said. Perhaps that's what led her mother to sign Florence up for a youth race in their hometown of Los Angeles, California, when she was only seven. From then on, Florence was hooked on track and field.

She ran throughout high school and joined the track team at California State University, Northridge, in 1979 before transferring to the University of California, Los Angeles, which had a renowned athletics program. Florence excelled over the next eight years, winning many titles and medals before taking a break to work at a bank and style nails and hair.

By then she was a media sensation, both for her running and her style. With her long hair, red lipstick, painted nails, and brightly colored one-legged unitards, she was a showstopper when she stepped on the track. But Florence was also quick to correct reporters who assumed her attention to glamour was more important to her than running, "I spend about fifteen minutes putting on my makeup. I spend a lot longer getting ready for a race."

When Florence hit the track at the 1988 US Olympic trials, she ran the 100-meter dash in 10.49 seconds—half a second faster than her personal best and .16 seconds faster than the previous record holder—and made history. Then, at the Olympics that year, she wowed the crowds by setting a world record of 21.34 seconds in the 200-meter dash. She ended up bringing home three gold medals and one silver.

FloJo died of a seizure in 1998, stunning the country and the world. Thirty-two years after her historic Olympics, no woman has broken her record.

JANET JACKSON

THE FIRST ARTIST TO HAVE SEVEN
TOP-FIVE HITS ON A SINGLE ALBUM (1989)

"

I would hope my legacy would be bringing smiles to faces.

"

Imagine having five of the most famous people in the world as your big brothers! Many people might have been intimidated or happy to fade into the background . . . but not Janet Damita Jo Jackson. In her legendary career, she has broken records that her brothers in the Jackson Five never achieved—and she did it all as the baby of the family.

At first, Janet wanted to race horses or be a lawyer when she grew up. She started acting as a teenager to make money to support those dreams but caught the entertainment bug after her roles on the sitcoms *Good Times* and *Diff'rent Strokes*. Janet even recorded two albums with her family's help. However, she knew she could be a success on her own.

In 1986, at age twenty, Janet fired her father as her manager and recorded the album *Control*. It went straight to the top of Billboard's bestselling albums chart. The album's themes of self-sufficiency reflected her growing into her own as an adult. In 1989 her album *Rhythm Nation 1814* took her message of empowerment even further. Janet voiced her opinions about poverty, racial injustice, and other important issues through music. Janet was only twenty-three, but she became the first artist in history to have an album produce seven top-five singles, something even her most famous sibling, Michael, couldn't do!

Today, with eleven albums under her belt and 160 million albums sold, Janet shows no sign of stopping. She can dance, sing, and act—but perhaps most importantly, she used her fame and power to challenge people's ideas of what young women could want and be.

OCTAVIA BUTLER

THE FIRST SCIENCE-FICTION WRITER
TO WIN A MACARTHUR FOUNDATION
"GENIUS" GRANT (1995)

"

TELL STORIES
filled with facts.
MAKE PEOPLE
TOUCH AND TASTE
AND KNOW.
Make people
FEEL! FEEL! FEEL!

"

In elementary school, Octavia Butler spent afternoons at the public library in her hometown of Pasadena, California, to evade the bullies who made fun of her. Soon, she finished all the books in the children's section and moved on to myths, legends, fantasy novels, and her favorite, science-fiction stories. Octavia loved the way the books broadened her imagination and took her away from a world that was not always kind.

There were no well-known black female science-fiction writers, so Octavia decided she would be the first. She often wrote encouraging notes to herself in her diary, like, "I [will] write best-selling novels . . . so be it! See to it!" Her first book, *Patternmaster*, was published in 1976, based on an idea she had when she was twelve. With its futuristic mind readers and mutants, it caused a stir by portraying flawed, complex characters whose struggles reflected the real world.

Books like the time-travel romance *Kindred* (1979) and *The Parable of the Sower* (1993), about a teen girl with metaphysical powers, became beloved by young and adult readers alike. In 1995, the MacArthur Foundation, whose mission is to help people and institutions build a more "just, verdant, and peaceful world," gave Octavia their famous Fellowship, the so-called Genius award. The foundation (not to mention Octavia's millions of fans and readers) believed that her "transcendent fables, which have as much to do with the future as with the present and the past" could change the world. Though other writers, like Leslie Marmon Silko, Ved Mehta, and May Swenson, had previously received the award, she was the first science-fiction writer ever to be honored.

In all, Octavia wrote twelve novels and dozens of stories and essays before her death in 2006. Her legacy lives on in various ways. A mountain on Charon (moon of Pluto) was named *Butler Mons* in her honor in 2018. The following year, the Los Angeles Public Library opened the Octavia Lab, a maker space and audiovisual space.

SELENA QUINTANILLA-PÉREZ

THE FIRST LATINX ARTIST TO HAVE A NUMBER ONE BILLBOARD 200 ALBUM (1995)

When Selena Quintanilla began to sing with her siblings at age six, her father, Abraham, was shocked—she had nearly perfect pitch and extraordinary control of her voice. Perhaps Abraham shouldn't have been surprised. Music seemed to run in the entire family's veins.

Selena and her siblings formed a band called Selena y Los Dinos, with her sister on drums and her brother on bass. They performed a style of Mexican American music called Tejano, which mixes strong rhythms with jazz, country, and polka. At sixteen, she won Best Female Vocalist of the Year at the 1987 Tejano Music Awards—and she was awarded the title for the next nine years!

Music continued to be a family affair as Selena's fame grew. She even married Chris Pérez, the guitarist from her band. She became known for her radiant smile, commitment to women's rights, and joyful performances to record-breaking audiences, earning the nickname "La Reina," or "The Queen." Selena's fifth album, *Dreaming of You*, debuted at number one on the Billboard 200 chart in August 1995, a few months after she was murdered at the age of twenty-three. It was the first recording by a Hispanic artist to do so, and it remains the bestselling Latin record of all time.

Selena's legacy was tragically cut short. But even after her death, she continued to break boundaries. A tribute concert by Los Dinos commemorating the tenth anniversary of her death was the most viewed Spanish-language television special in American history. And she is often credited with opening the door for Latinx artists such as Ricky Martin and Selena Gomez to succeed in the United States.

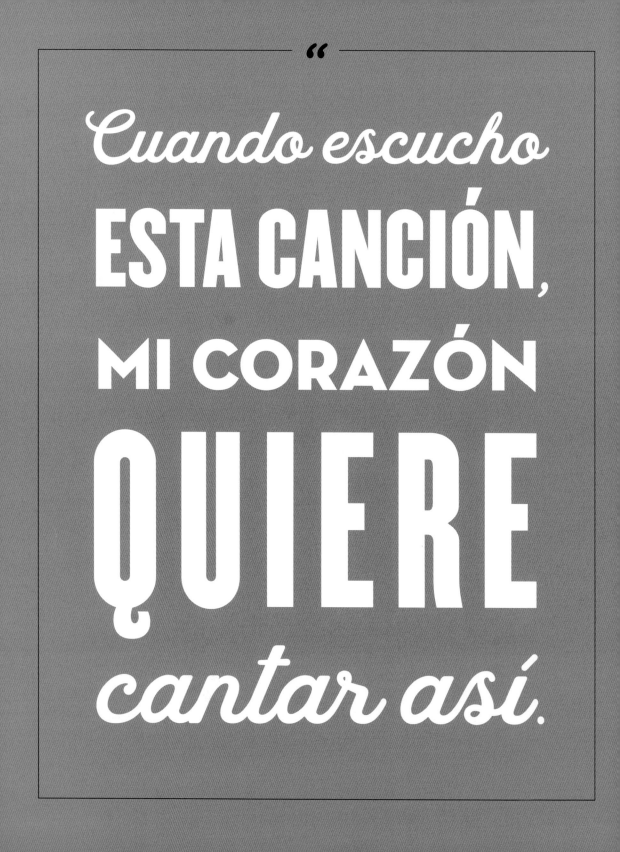

"

Cuando escucho
ESTA CANCIÓN,
MI CORAZÓN
QUIERE
cantar así.

When I hear THIS SONG, MY HEART WANTS TO SING like this.

"

—SELENA QUINTANILLA-PÉREZ

MICHAEL JORDAN

THE FIRST PLAYER TO BE NAMED
THE NBA'S ROOKIE OF THE YEAR,
DEFENSIVE PLAYER OF THE YEAR,
NBA MVP, ALL-STAR MVP,
AND FINALS MVP (1996)

In sports like track or tennis, it's easy to tell who won the race or match. It is more difficult to identify the best player in team sports . . . unless the sport is basketball and the player is Michael Jordan, hailed as the greatest basketball player of all time. One ESPN survey ranked him as the greatest athlete of the twentieth century.

Funnily enough, when Michael was a sophomore in high school, he tried out for the varsity basketball team and was rejected for being too short! Michael took that early failure as a challenge, and by the time he shot up to his full height of six foot six, he was fielding offers from top college basketball programs around the country.

Michael had an all-court game—he could jump higher than most of his competitors and defended the perimeters of the court with ease. After graduating from the University of North Carolina–Chapel Hill in 1984, he was drafted by the Chicago Bulls as a shooting guard and was named Rookie of the Year after his first season. He was an early fan favorite, and in the 1986 season he became the second player in history to score over 3,000 points in a season.

"Air Jordan" continued to prove himself on the court year after year, and none more so than the 1995–1996 season. That year saw Michael named the All-Star Most Valuable Player, Finals MVP, and the NBA's overall MVP, making him the first player ever to achieve those honors plus Rookie of the Year (1985) and Defensive Player of the Year (1988). Under Michael's reign, NBA basketball became one of the United States' greatest exports, as fans all over the world tuned in to see what he would accomplish next.

Michael retired in 2003 but kept racking up "firsts." The NBA's first billionaire player, he's also the first African American or former player to own a majority stake in a basketball team. His philosophy is that you'll always get better as long as you try. He said, "I've missed more than 9,000 shots in my career . . . I've failed over and over and over again in my life. And that is why I succeed."

ELLEN DEGENERES

THE FIRST PERSON TO PLAY A GAY LEAD CHARACTER ON NETWORK TELEVISION (1997)

> "
> *Never follow anyone else's path, unless you're in the woods and you're lost and you see a path. Then by all means, follow that path.*
> "

Louisiana native Ellen DeGeneres hosts a top-rated talk show and has starred in sitcoms, recorded stand-up comedy specials, hosted awards shows, written books, and founded charities. But young Ellen wanted to be a songwriter. She had a knack for observing moments that others might have missed. "I watch people's behavior and notice things," she explained when asked about her start. "I started writing songs, and that turned into comedy."

Ellen's personal life became very public on April 14, 1997, when she came out as a lesbian to *Time* magazine. The cover showed a grinning Ellen with a headline in bright red letters: *Yep, I'm Gay!* At the same time, the character she was playing on the sitcom *Ellen* also came out, making her the first gay lead on American network TV.

Her actions helped normalize homosexuality at a time when gay people couldn't marry legally and were denied other civil rights. In 2016, President Obama even awarded her a Presidential Medal of Freedom in honor of her groundbreaking decision to live openly and for showing others "that a single individual can make the world a more fun, more open, more loving place."

In 2003, Ellen began hosting *The Ellen DeGeneres Show*. Her goal for the program? "Our only agenda is to make people feel good," she said. With thirty Emmys, twenty People's Choice Awards, nine Teen Choice Awards, and nominations for Grammys and Golden Globes, Ellen has succeeded by being herself: a force for warm, friendly fun in Hollywood and around the world.

MERYL STREEP

THE FIRST PERSON TO BE NOMINATED
FOR THIRTEEN OSCARS (2003)

> "
> *The formula of happiness and success is just being actually yourself, in the most vivid possible way you can.*
> "

It might come as a surprise that one of Hollywood's most-awarded actors never wanted to be a movie star at all. Young Mary Louise Streep studied opera and was a cheerleader, but only discovered her passion for acting while attending Vassar College. After she graduated from the Yale School of Drama in 1975, Meryl (as she was now called) preferred performing live in works by great writers such as Shakespeare and Chekhov. She hated seeing herself on-screen, and after her first try, pledged to never make another film. Robert De Niro, a famous actor friend, convinced her to try again in a movie called *The Deer Hunter*. That role earned Meryl a nomination for her first Academy Award, and almost despite herself, she was soon on the path to film superstardom.

In 2003, she was nominated for the Academy Award for Best Supporting Actress for her role in *Adaptation*—her thirteenth nomination—making her the most-nominated performer in the Academy's history, topping the previous record shared by Katharine Hepburn and Jack Nicholson.

Audiences love to see Meryl's transformations on-screen, from an icy magazine editor in *The Devil Wears Prada* to the British prime minister Margaret Thatcher in *The Iron Lady*. Seventy-six movies and nineteen television shows later, her philosophy is that "acting has to reach everybody on some level—it's a communication of feeling." Sure enough, Meryl has garnered continued love from the Academy Awards—she currently has twenty-one nominations (including three wins!).

MIUCCIA PRADA

THE FIRST WOMAN TO WIN A CFDA INTERNATIONAL AWARD (2004)

"

Fashion is instant language.

"

As a child, Miuccia Prada learned her family's history by heart. In 1913, her grandfather founded the Prada brand in Milan, Italy, selling suitcases, shoes, and bags in Galleria Vittorio, the oldest shopping center in the world. By the time Miuccia was born in 1949, the family business was the official leather goods supplier to the Italian royal household.

Miuccia loved her grandfather's story, but she also had other interests. In college, she studied drama and politics, and after receiving her PhD in political science, she spent five years as a mime! When she took her mother's place as the head of Prada, Miuccia found she had a knack for the business. Many of her former intellectual and activist friends found luxury goods and runway fashion to be frivolous and elitist. But Miuccia refused to compromise either her intellectual principles

or her love for her family's heritage. She believed her designs could change the world.

Her breakthrough moment came in 1985, with Prada's trademark nylon backpack. Made of fabric from a parachute factory in the same way one might treat expensive fabrics like silk or cashmere, the simple bags felt modern. They became must-haves and sparked questions about how fashion could be more useful and accessible for everyone.

As lead creative director and co–chief executive officer of Prada, Miuccia has continued to innovate fashion. It was no surprise when the Council of Fashion Designers of America made her the first female designer to win the International Award in 2004. Rather than trying to fit a mold created by her family, she chose to be herself, making Prada one of the richest and most powerful fashion brands in the world.

J. K. ROWLING

THE FIRST BILLIONAIRE AUTHOR (2004)

Growing up in Gloucestershire, England, Joanne Kathleen Rowling (or "Jo") was a quiet child who loved spinning stories for her sister. Jo never stopped coming up with stories, and one idea in particular—about a boy who realizes he belongs to a world of wizards—had taken root in her brain. But life as a grown-up was filled with challenges. After the death of her mother and a painful breakup, she was without a job and struggling to support her young daughter. Still, she knew that she had to share her magical idea.

That idea became *Harry Potter and the Philosopher's Stone* (published as *Harry Potter and the Sorcerer's Stone* in North America). Almost before Jo could say "*stupefy*," she was being offered about two million dollars for the chance to make the first four books into movies. Now the books in the Harry Potter series have been published in over eighty languages, with more than five hundred million copies sold. In 2004, *Forbes* magazine reported that Jo was the first author ever to earn more than a billion dollars from book sales and projects related to their writings.

Generosity and the importance of sticking up for the underdog were not only values she wove into her tales, but were also strong values in her life. By 2012, she could no longer claim to be a billionaire as she had given away around $160 million to charities supporting families, literacy, and research on diseases like multiple sclerosis. To her, the most magical outcome of the success of the Harry Potter series is that it not only allowed her to help other people, but also encouraged her readers to do the same.

"

WE DO NOT NEED MAGIC
to transform
THE WORLD.

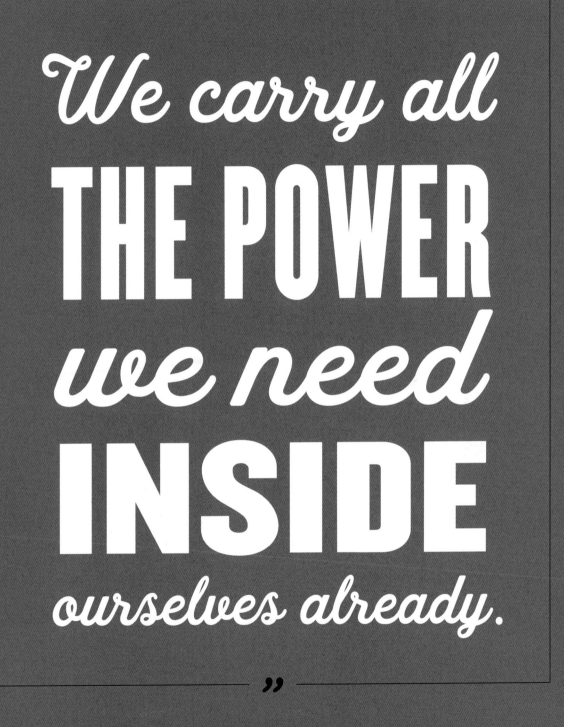

We carry all
THE POWER
we need
INSIDE
ourselves already.
„

— J. K. ROWLING

ANG LEE

THE FIRST PERSON OF COLOR TO WIN THE ACADEMY AWARD FOR BEST DIRECTOR (2005)

> "
> *Filmmaking is my alter ego. I'm the Hulk.*
> *I'm the hidden dragon . . . The movies possess me.*
> "

Young Ang Lee was a good boy, who never thought about breaking the rules. His father, Sheng, and mother, Se-Tsung, had left China after a violent civil war and settled in Taiwan to give their children a better life. Their dreams for Ang were of safety, security, and scholarly excellence.

But Ang twice failed the entrance exam to the Chinese school his father hoped he would attend, and instead graduated from an arts school. He then moved to the US to study acting. But when he took the stage, his Chinese accent didn't fit with his teachers' ideas of how an actor should sound.

That was when Ang turned to directing. After helming several films in Taiwan, he got his first big international break directing *Sense and Sensibility* (1995). The movie was nominated for seven Academy Awards. More films and accolades followed, including *Crouching Tiger, Hidden Dragon* (2000), which won the Academy Award for Best Foreign Language Film, and *Hulk* (2003). Though his career was very different from his parents' original hopes for him, they were deeply proud of all he achieved.

It was *Brokeback Mountain*, a movie about two cowboys who fall in love, that earned Ang the Academy Award for Best Director in 2005. He was the first Asian person and the first person of color to win the trophy. In his speech, he thanked his father for the influence he had on Ang's life. "More than any other, I made [*Brokeback Mountain*] for him." Ang would win the award again in 2012 for his work on *Life of Pi*.

CESAR CHAVEZ

THE FIRST MEXICAN AMERICAN TO HAVE A NATIONAL HOLIDAY NAMED AFTER HIM (2014)

The son of immigrants—his parents and grandparents had immigrated to Texas from Mexico—Cesar Chavez and his family moved constantly. Like many migrant workers during the Great Depression, they went where there was work. By eighth grade, Cesar was picking fruit full-time to help support his family.

After fighting in World War II, he was horrified to see that conditions for farm workers hadn't changed. Pesticides were making families sick. Often, there weren't schools for workers' kids. The growers could be abusive. It made Cesar angry, but by then he had begun reading the work of St. Francis of Assisi, Mahatma Gandhi, and Dr. Martin Luther King, Jr. Their writings advocated for peaceful solutions to injustice. Cesar believed the US could—and should—be a great place for all people.

He moved to California to cofound (with Dolores Huerta) what became the United Farm Workers (UFW). Their mission was simple: "to bring about social justice for the men, women, and children who work to provide the food we eat." Cesar fought to help workers improve their lives, and his efforts paid off. By the 1970s, over seventeen million Americans were boycotting the products of companies that treated their workers unfairly.

Cesar received the United States' highest civilian award, the Presidential Medal of Freedom, one year after he died, in 1994. Twenty years later, President Barack Obama proclaimed March 31 Cesar Chavez Day. He was the first Mexican American ever to be given such an honor.

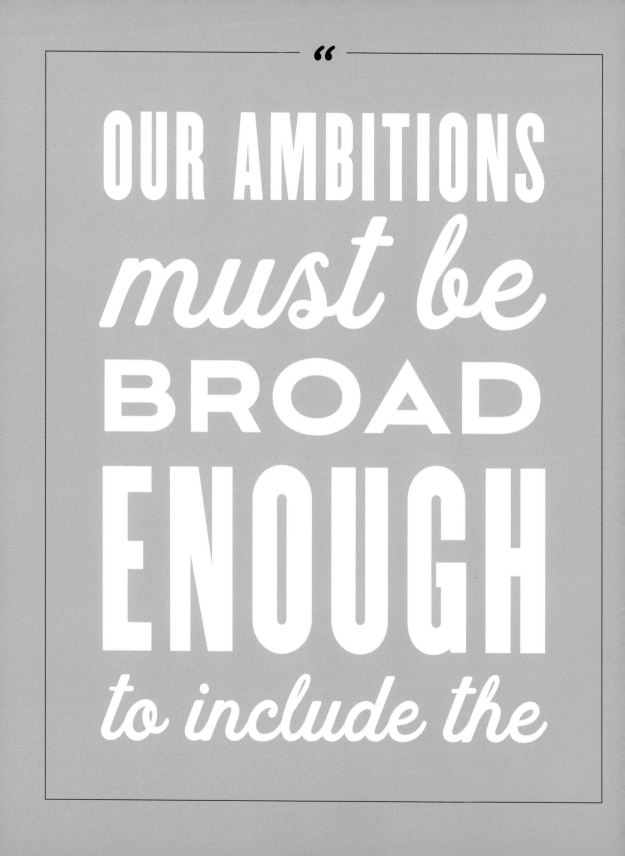

"

OUR AMBITIONS
must be
BROAD
ENOUGH
to include the

ASPIRATIONS
and needs
OF OTHERS,
FOR THEIR SAKES,
and for our own.

"

—CESAR CHAVEZ

LAVERNE COX

THE FIRST OPENLY TRANSGENDER PERSON TO BE NOMINATED FOR AN ACTING EMMY (2014)

> "
> *By doing the work to love ourselves more,*
> *I believe we will love each other better.*
> "

Laverne Cox was a dancer during her childhood in Mobile, Alabama, eventually attending a prestigious arts high school and moving to New York City to get a degree in dance. She dreamed of making it on Broadway, so Laverne was surprised when her first big break came from a reality TV show, *I Want to Work for Diddy*. She became a fan favorite and used the platform to get a starring role on her own show, *TRANSform Me*.

Over the next few years, she booked only small parts. But it was her history-making role on the show *Orange Is the New Black* as Sophia Burset that made her perhaps the most famous trans woman in America and a media superstar—she appeared on magazine covers, talk shows, and red carpets worldwide. She became the first openly trans actor to be nominated for an acting Emmy Award in 2014.

That same year, she produced a documentary called *Laverne Cox Presents: The T Word*. When she won the 2015 Daytime Emmy Award in Outstanding Special Class Special for it, she became the first trans woman to win a producing Emmy, as well.

Laverne has spoken often about the responsibility she feels for the trans community, especially transgender women of color. As a new generation of trans actresses like Hari Nef, Indya Moore, and Janet Mock see success in Hollywood, Cox serves as an example of a Hollywood dynamo who has succeeded not because or in spite of her gender identity, but because of her radiant star power and talent.

AUDRA MCDONALD

THE FIRST PERSON TO WIN THE TONY AWARD IN ALL FOUR ACTING CATEGORIES (2014)

> "
> *If I could ask God one question, it would be:*
> *Can I perform in heaven?*
> "

As a child in Fresno, California, Audra McDonald loved to sing. She could perform pop songs and operatic pieces with the same skill. Her first big role after graduating from New York's famed Juilliard School was in *Carousel*, which earned her a Tony Award (the biggest award you can win in American theater) for Best Featured Actress in a Musical in 1994. More awards quickly followed; by 1998, she had won two more Tonys.

From playing the Mother Superior in *The Sound of Music* to Bess in *The Gershwins' Porgy and Bess*, Audra infused her roles with thoughtfulness and passion. She was a shining example of how theater could benefit from hiring performers of all racial backgrounds. As Audra told the *New York Times*, "If I think I am right for a role, I will go for it in whatever way I can. I refuse to say no to myself."

In 2014, Audra made history when she won the Tony Award for Best Performance by a Leading Actress in a Play for her role as Billie Holiday in *Lady Day at Emerson's Bar and Grill*. That win made her the first performer to win Tonys in all acting categories—Best Featured Actress in a Play, Best Featured Actress in a Musical, Best Actress in a Play, and Best Actress in a Musical. (She is also the first performer to win six Tony Awards.) In her acceptance speech, she tearfully thanked the "strong and brave and courageous" African American women of theater who paved the way for her. Just like them, Audra McDonald will go down in history as a performer who used her talents to the utmost.

MISTY COPELAND

THE FIRST BLACK PRINCIPAL BALLERINA
AT AMERICAN BALLET THEATRE (2015)

> " *I can do anything when I am in a tutu.* "

As a child, Misty Copeland was small and thin and very shy. When she first took a ballet class at the Boys & Girls Club in San Pedro, California, no one expected her to one day be a star.

But Misty's gift for ballet was something extraordinary. Her teachers encouraged her to follow her dream of dancing with America's national ballet company, American Ballet Theatre (ABT). Despite her skill and enthusiasm for dance, the world of elite dance companies often could feel very far away. Misty was one of six children, and though her mother worked hard to support them all, for a while, they were homeless and shared a small room in a motel.

Still, Misty kept training. She earned a spot in ABT's studio company in New York City in 2000 and dreamed of becoming a principal ballerina. These dancers are the ones who perform the most challenging roles. In its history, ABT had never had a black principal ballerina. Despite others' racism and her own self-doubt, Misty held tight to her dream of being the first as she mastered famous roles in ballets such as *Swan Lake* and *Romeo and Juliet*. Why did she work so hard? "I think that's my purpose: to bring people in, to make them feel like they belong," she said.

On June 30, 2015, Misty became the first African American to be named principal ballerina—the highest rank a dancer can achieve—in the history of ABT. Her triumph made the headlines of newspapers worldwide. But for Misty, the honor was about more than making history; it was about helping everyone feel welcome in the world of ballet.

DOLLY PARTON

THE FIRST PERSON TO HAVE TOP 20 HITS
IN SIX DECADES (2016)

Dolly Parton's talent as a songwriter is legendary, though few would have guessed that the East Tennessee mountain girl would one day become one of the best-selling country music artists of all time.

Born in 1946, Dolly was one of twelve kids. Her parents were sharecroppers who worked wealthier people's land, and they didn't have a lot of money to spare. She dreamed of becoming rich and famous to help her family . . . and she wouldn't have to wait long. She was writing her own music and lyrics by the age of five, recorded her first album at ten, and began performing her own compositions at Nashville, Tennessee's Grand Ole Opry (a radio show broadcast worldwide from the most famous stage in country music) when she was only thirteen years old.

Six decades later, Dolly's bright soprano voice, rhinestone costumes, glittery makeup, and trademark blond hair light up the stage just as radiantly as ever. By 2008, forty of her albums had reached the top 10 on the Billboard Country charts—a feat that still hasn't been matched by any other woman. And in 2016, she became the first person to have had one of her songs—which meld gospel, bluegrass, country, and pop—reach the top 20 on the music charts in every decade since the 1960s.

Dolly still writes every day, and she estimates she's written over 3,000 songs. Beyond music, she has also acted in popular films like *9 to 5* and *Steel Magnolias*, and she even has her own theme park, Dollywood. "I want to be accepted myself, and I not only accept, but celebrate, the difference in everyone," Dolly has said, and for her many fans, she's become a symbol of loving yourself and others, rhinestones and all.

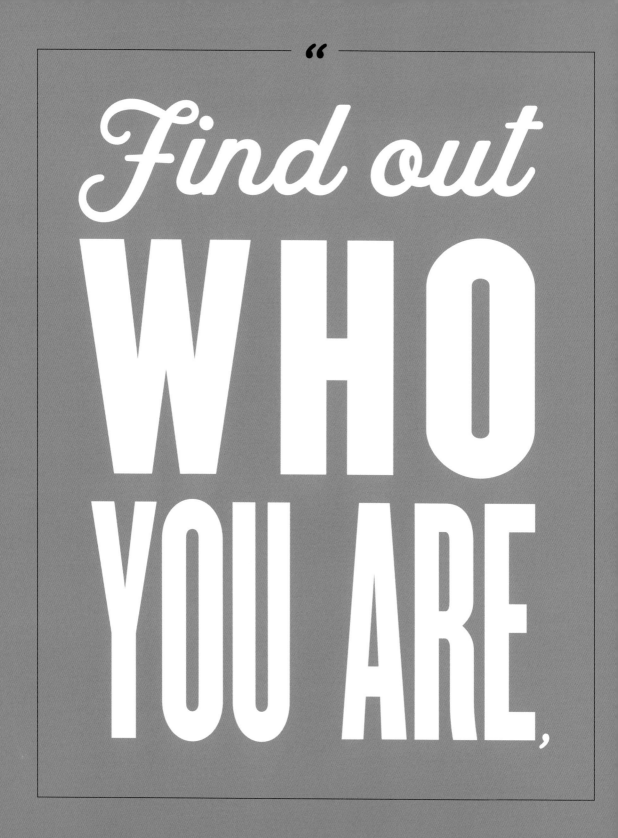

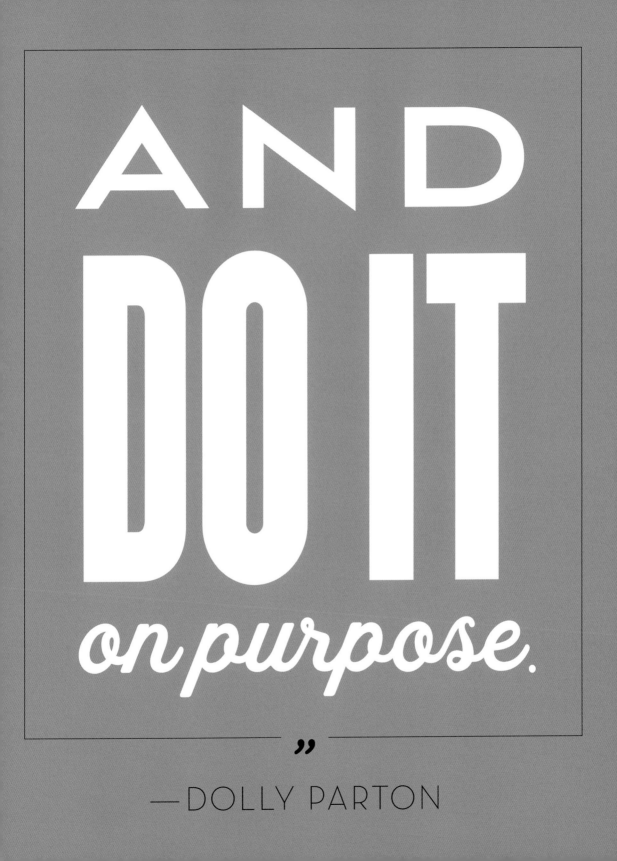

AND
DO IT
on purpose.

"

— DOLLY PARTON

BOB DYLAN

THE FIRST SONGWRITER TO RECEIVE THE NOBEL PRIZE FOR LITERATURE (2016)

> *People listen to my songs and they must think I'm a certain type of way, and maybe I am. But there's more to it than that. I think they can listen to my songs and figure out who they are, too.*

Robert Zimmerman was a boy in Minnesota when he discovered rock and roll. He loved the way the music made his emotions feel richer, more real. He learned guitar by listening to the greats of rock, blues, and country, and dreamed of touring the world.

In college, Robert changed his name to "Bob Dylan." Melding folk and African American spirituals with the songs he had grown up with, Bob wrote about the quickly changing and sometimes frightening world of the 1960s. In songs like "The Times They Are a Changin'" and "Like a Rolling Stone," he paired his thoughts about war, civil rights, and unemployment with melodies.

Some audiences thought Bob wanted to stir up trouble with his lyrics. But as he later said, though his songs reflected his progressive mindset, he hoped the music would still make people dance, sing, and feel. Newspapers began calling him "the voice of his generation," and indeed, with thirty-eight albums to his name, few musicians have had a career as storied as his.

The Nobel Prize is given yearly to the people at the top of their fields. No songwriter had ever received the prestigious literature prize before . . . until Bob. In 2016, he was awarded the Nobel Prize in Literature "for having created new poetic expressions within the great American song tradition." Like books, plays, or poetry, his body of work had used the power of words to change the world.

JEAN-MICHEL BASQUIAT

THE FIRST AMERICAN ARTIST WHOSE ARTWORK
SOLD FOR OVER $110 MILLION (2017)

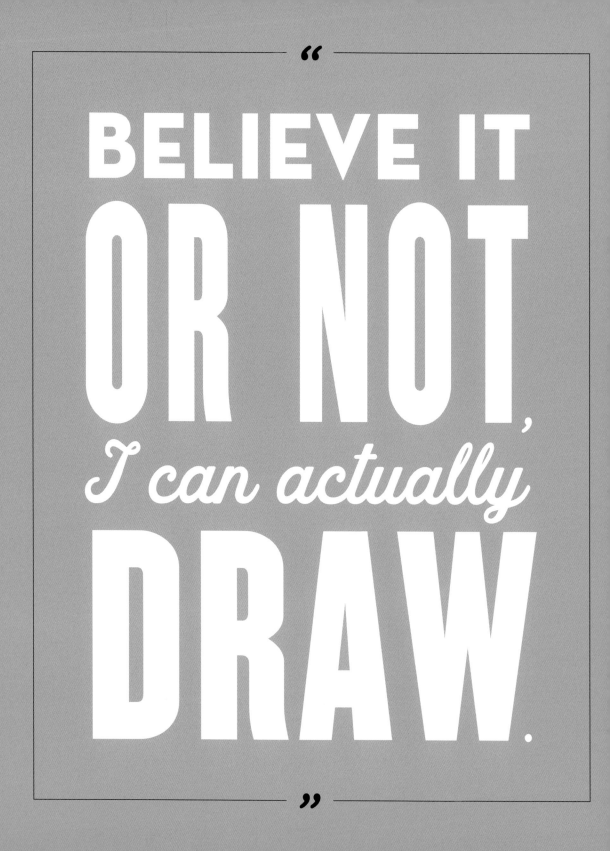

Jean-Michel Basquiat was born in New York to art-loving Haitian and Puerto Rican parents. His mother would often walk with him to the Brooklyn Museum, where he became a junior member. When he was eight, Jean-Michel was hit by a car and struggled to understand what had happened to his body. His mother bought him a copy of an illustrated medical book called *Gray's Anatomy*. He pored over the pages, fascinated by the drawings of bones and muscles. He decided he wanted to be an artist, too.

At age seventeen, Jean-Michel and a friend began painting graffiti on the sides of buildings. He sold his first painting in 1980 for two hundred dollars to a musician named Debbie Harry after he appeared in a music video for her band, Blondie.

Jean-Michel was a member of the neo-expressionist art movement, attempting to make art that could express emotion through color and composition. He would paint pictures of famous black male athletes, writers, and musicians, often adorning the skull-like heads with crowns to show his admiration. Painted on canvases, fences, and even the sides of buildings, his bold lines and overlapping words and images may not have made his subjects *look* true to life, but they *felt* real.

Jean-Michel struggled with drugs and depression, and in 1988, at the age of twenty-seven, he died of a drug overdose. But his fame continued to grow as his work began to be collected in museums worldwide. In May 2017, his painting *Untitled* (1982) sold for an unprecedented $110.5 million at an art auction. Never before had an American painting been valued so highly. The sale helped cement his legacy, and put him in the league of artists like Leonardo da Vinci and Pablo Picasso.

RUPAUL CHARLES

THE FIRST DRAG QUEEN TO GET A STAR
ON THE HOLLYWOOD WALK OF FAME (2018)

"

Don't be afraid to use all the colors in the crayon box.

"

In 1975, RuPaul Charles left San Diego for Atlanta with two goals: he wanted to be famous, and he wanted to break all the entertainment industry's rules. He also hoped to create more room for people to express themselves. He became an expert at the art of drag, or someone of one gender dressing and performing as another in creative ways.

When RuPaul danced and sang, people couldn't look away. He was approached to appear in films and advertisements. The makeup brand MAC Cosmetics hired him to be the face of the company in 1994; the campaign brought his message of self-acceptance all over the world. RuPaul recorded songs like "Supermodel (You Better Work)" and "Glamazon" that hit the top of the dance charts, and his self-titled television show (RuPaul was the first drag queen to ever host a national TV show) featured interviews with famous friends like Diana Ross, Cher, and Mary J. Blige.

Though he was long beloved by the LGBTQIA+ community, RuPaul was still relatively unknown to wider audiences. That changed when he began producing and hosting his own drag-themed reality competition in 2009, the Emmy Award–winning *RuPaul's Drag Race*, which now airs all over the world. The young man from San Diego had achieved his goals, and then some. In 2018, he became the first drag queen to get a star on the Hollywood Walk of Fame.

Now, even more than fame and rebellion, he has come to relish inspiring others to embrace their own fabulous identities. In his own words, "If you can't love yourself, how . . . you gonna love somebody else?"

BEYONCÉ KNOWLES-CARTER

THE FIRST BLACK WOMAN TO HEADLINE COACHELLA (2018)

"

Do what you were born to do. You have to trust yourself.

"

Beyoncé has lived a life of firsts. She was the first black woman to win the Pop Songwriter of the Year award. She was the first female artist to win six Grammys in one night. And she was the first act in history to have her first six solo albums debut at number one on the Billboard 200 chart. Her determination to break barriers has inspired her fans to crown their leader "Queen Bey."

At age five, Beyoncé saw Michael Jackson sing and dance onstage, lights flashing and crowd screaming. She knew then that she wanted to bring that kind of joy to people around the world. At fifteen, she and three friends formed the band Destiny's Child, which became one of the most successful music acts of the 2000s. But as Beyoncé later said, "I'm not happy if I'm

not improving, evolving, moving forward, inspiring, teaching, and learning." Beyoncé released her first solo album in 2003, which has since sold over eleven million records worldwide. Her 2016 hit song "Formation" lays out the recipe for her record-breaking success: "I dream it, I work hard, I grind till I own it."

Every year in California, almost half a million people gather at one of the biggest music festivals in the world: Coachella. No black woman had ever been chosen as the headlining act before 2018, when Beyoncé took the stage with a performance honoring her African American heritage. One hundred twenty-five thousand fans (plus another forty-one million viewers online!) sang and danced along, just as she believed they would when she was a young girl.

What will YOU BE THE FIRST TO DO?

WHO DID IT FIRST?
ACROSS TIME

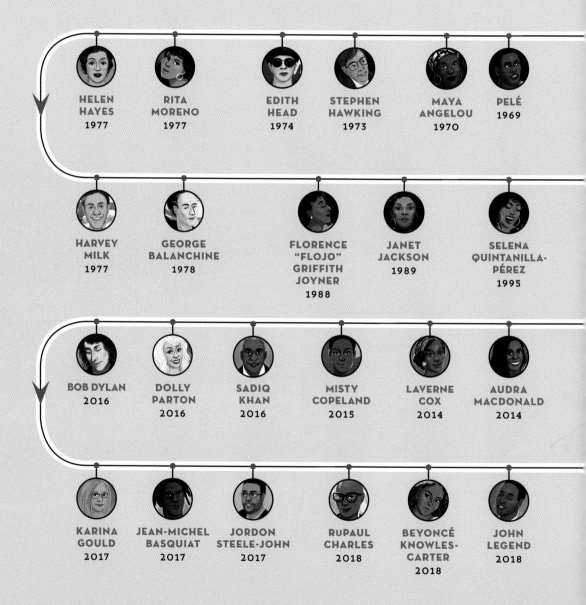

HELEN HAYES 1977

RITA MORENO 1977

EDITH HEAD 1974

STEPHEN HAWKING 1973

MAYA ANGELOU 1970

PELÉ 1969

HARVEY MILK 1977

GEORGE BALANCHINE 1978

FLORENCE "FLOJO" GRIFFITH JOYNER 1988

JANET JACKSON 1989

SELENA QUINTANILLA-PÉREZ 1995

BOB DYLAN 2016

DOLLY PARTON 2016

SADIQ KHAN 2016

MISTY COPELAND 2015

LAVERNE COX 2014

AUDRA MACDONALD 2014

KARINA GOULD 2017

JEAN-MICHEL BASQUIAT 2017

JORDON STEELE-JOHN 2017

RUPAUL CHARLES 2018

BEYONCÉ KNOWLES-CARTER 2018

JOHN LEGEND 2018

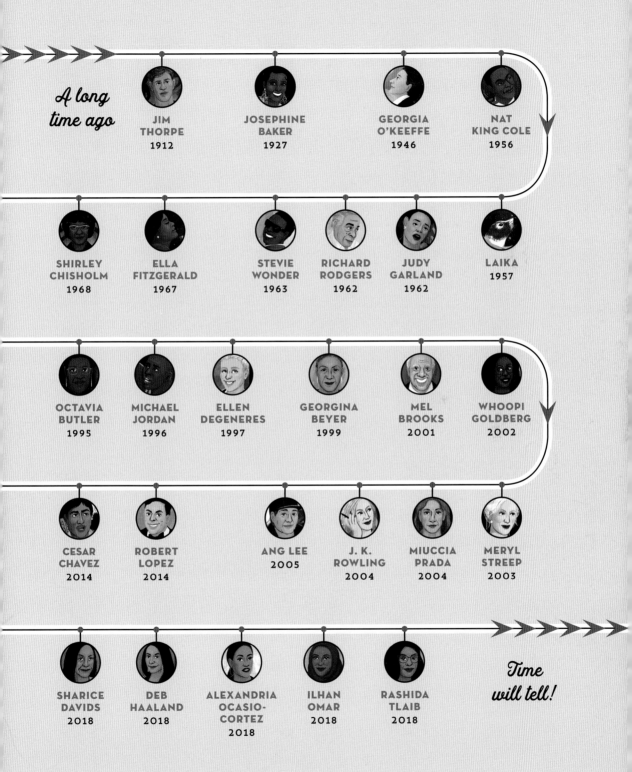

A long time ago

JIM THORPE
1912

JOSEPHINE BAKER
1927

GEORGIA O'KEEFFE
1946

NAT KING COLE
1956

SHIRLEY CHISHOLM
1968

ELLA FITZGERALD
1967

STEVIE WONDER
1963

RICHARD RODGERS
1962

JUDY GARLAND
1962

LAIKA
1957

OCTAVIA BUTLER
1995

MICHAEL JORDAN
1996

ELLEN DEGENERES
1997

GEORGINA BEYER
1999

MEL BROOKS
2001

WHOOPI GOLDBERG
2002

CESAR CHAVEZ
2014

ROBERT LOPEZ
2014

ANG LEE
2005

J. K. ROWLING
2004

MIUCCIA PRADA
2004

MERYL STREEP
2003

SHARICE DAVIDS
2018

DEB HAALAND
2018

ALEXANDRIA OCASIO-CORTEZ
2018

ILHAN OMAR
2018

RASHIDA TLAIB
2018

Time will tell!

FURTHER EXPLORATION

The profiles in this book tell only part of these icons' stories. Here are some suggested resources for further reading, listening, and watching to learn more about their lives and work.

BOOKS

Arp, Robert, et al, editors. *The Philosophy of Ang Lee*. The University Press of Kentucky, 2013.

Brown, Monica. *Pelé: King of Soccer / Pelé: El rey del fútbol*. Illustrated by Rudy Gutiérrez, HarperCollins, 2017.

Caswell, Kurt. *Laika's Window: The Legacy of a Soviet Space Dog*. Trinity University Press, 2019.

Copeland, Misty. *Life in Motion: An Unlikely Ballerina*. Aladdin, 2018.

Dionne, Evette. *Lifting As We Climb: Black Women's Battle for the Ballot Box*. Penguin Young Readers Group, 2020.

Dylan, Bob. *The Lyrics: 1961–2012*. Simon & Schuster, 2016.

Epstein, Daniel Mark. *Nat King Cole*. Farrar, Straus and Giroux, 1999.

Hawking, Lucy, and Stephen Hawking. *George's Secret Key to the Universe*. Simon & Schuster Books for Young Readers, 2007.

Hegedus, Bethany. *Rise!: From Caged Bird to Poet of the People, Maya Angelou*. Illustrated by Tonya Engel, Lee & Low Books Inc., 2019.

Jorgensen, Jay. *Edith Head: The Fifty-Year Career of Hollywood's Greatest Costume Designer*. Introduction by Sandy Powell, Running Press, 2010.

Krull, Kathleen. *Harvesting Hope: The Story of Cesar Chavez*. Illustrated by Yuyi Morales, Houghton Mifflin Harcourt, 2003.

Novesky, Amy. *Georgia in Hawaii: When Georgia O'Keeffe Painted What She Pleased*. Illustrated by Yuyi Morales, Harcourt Children's Books, 2012.

Ottaviani, Jim. *Hawking*. Illustrated by Leland Myrick, First Second, 2019.

Parton, Dolly. *Coat of Many Colors*. Illustrated by Judith Sutton, HarperTrophy, 1996.

Powell, Patricia Hruby. *Josephine: the Dazzling Life of Josephine Baker*. Illustrated by Christian Robinson, Chronicle Books, 2014.

Rodríguez, Patty, et al. *The Life of Selena / La vida de Selena*. Lil' Libros, 2018.

Sanders, Rob. *Pride: The Story of Harvey Milk and the Rainbow Flag*. Illustrated by Steven Salerno, Random House, 2018.

Sheinkin, Steve. *Undefeated: Jim Thorpe and the Carlisle Indian School Football Team*. Roaring Brook Press, 2017.

Shapiro, Marc. *J. K. Rowling: The Wizard Behind Harry Potter*. St. Martin's Griffin, 2007.

Steptoe, Javaka. *Radiant Child: The Story of Young Artist Jean-Michel Basquiat*. Little, Brown Books for Young Readers, 2016.

Venable, Alan. *Flo Jo: The Story of Florence Griffith Joyner*. Don Johnston, Inc., 1999.

WEBSITES

"American Masters: George Balanchine—Master of the Dance." PBS.January 14, 2004. https://www.pbs.org/wnet/americanmasters/george-balanchine-master-of-the-dance/529/

Delaney, Jodi. "The Interviews: RuPaul Charles." Television Academy. July 24, 2019. www.emmys.com/news/interviews-archive/interviews-rupaul-charles.

Gans, Andrew. "Diva Talk: A Chat with Four-Time Tony Winner Audra McDonald." *Playbill*, December 24, 2004. www.playbill.com/article/diva-talk-a-chat-with-four-time-tony-winner-audra-mcdonald-com-123275.

"Halfback 'World's Greatest Athlete' Jim Thorpe." Pro Football Hall of Fame Official Site. www.profootballhof.com/players/jim-thorpe/.

"Miuccia Prada | BoF 500." *The Business of Fashion*. Accessed August 9, 2019. www.businessoffashion.com/community/people/miuccia-prada.

NBA.com Staff. "Legends Profile: Michael Jordan." NBA.com. August 25, 2017. www.nba.com/history/legends/profiles/michael-jordan.

"Octavia E. Butler: Telling My Stories." *The Huntington*. www.huntington.org /octavia-butler.

Rothman, Lily. "Ellen DeGeneres Coming Out Interview: 20th Anniversary." *Time*. April 13, 2017. time.com/4728994/ellen-degeneres-1997-coming-out-cover/.

Webber, Esther. "London Mayor: The Sadiq Khan Story." *BBC News*. May 7, 2016. www.bbc.com/news/uk-england-london-36140479.

VIDEOS, DOCUMENTARIES, AND ALBUMS

Beyoncé. *The Lion King: The Gift*. Parkwood Entertainment, Columbia Records, 2019.

"Brief But Spectacular: Rita Moreno, Actress and Singer." *PBS News Hour*, Public Broadcasting Service. www.pbs.org/newshour/brief/165270/rita-moreno.

Ella Fitzgerald. *Ella Fitzgerald Sings the Cole Porter Song Book*, Verve, UMG Recordings, 1997.

John Legend and the Roots. *Wake Up!*. Getting Out Our Dreams and Sony Music Entertainment, 2010.

Logue, Siobhan, dir. *Stevie Wonder: A Musical History*. BBC 4. 2019. https://www.bbc.co.uk/programmes/b0bss4sq.

Marshall, Rob, dir. *Into the Woods*. Walt Disney Studios Home Entertainment, 2014.

ALEX HART is the pseudonym for a children's book editor and author who is the first person in his family to write and publish a book. He lives with his husband in Brooklyn, New York, and Hillsdale, New York.

MEGAN REID works in books and television, and is the author of two other nonfiction titles for adults and kids. A child of Jamaican immigrants, she is the first person in her family to work for a Fortune 500 company. She lives and writes in Brooklyn, New York.

MEGANREID.CO

JESS CRUICKSHANK is an Australian illustrator and letterer based in Kitchener, Ontario. While she has created numerous book covers for publishers around the world, *Who Did It First? 50 Icons, Luminaries, and Legends Who Revolutionized the World* is her first fully illustrated children's book. She is the first person in her family to have participated in a televised spelling bee.

JESSCRUICKSHANK.COM